Rented Hearts

Christopher Jones

BookLeaf Publishing

Presentation by *BookLeaf Publishing*

Web: www.bookleafpub.com

E-mail: info@bookleafpub.com

ISBN: 9789357212007

First edition 2023

DEDICATION

Mum, love you lots, stop worrying, I'll always be ok. X

Brian,I hope I'm making your proud, I can only try to be as good as of a man as you were. X

Zowie, my paramour, my muse, it always has and always will be you xxx

ACKNOWLEDGEMENT

Bolton, Chorley, Wakefield, Malton, Ingleton, Whitby, Richmond, I've loved, I've lost, I've cried, I've laughed, I’ve learnt, but most of all I've found myself in each of these places, and for that I'm truly thankful, whether you broke me or made me, I’m me.

Christopher Jones
November 2022
Cover art by Emma Louise Lacy

PREFACE

"I would die a thousand deaths, if she was waiting for me every time"
Heathclff, Wuthering Heights
Imagine waiting 20 years for someone, the perfect person, imagine how it feels to finally hold them, share your life with them, imagine the love that you both share.
Now imagine that love being taken away in an instant.
This book comes from that instant moment, it's raw, it's painful, it's love gone wrong.

The Door

I unlock the door and walk into the empty abyss of our broken home, I feel you here, I hear you here, I pray that you are in our room, I push the door open, the lack of your presence makes my already rotting heart crumble more.

The Sound

The piercing sound of your absence is so loud, it forces my eyes to bleed your memory.

The Memory

Your memory burns my cheeks, when I think it
was everything, turned to nothing, the acidic
burn of loveless tears scars my face, just like
your goodbye scared my heart.

The Collision

When two hurricanes collide, the only damage done, is to each other.

The Vortex

My imperfect quietness, my silence, my slumber
and sleep, my nothingness, my swirling vortex
of broken peace, is shattered even more by the
loudness of your no reply

The condemned

Like a condemned man walking the green lit mile to his ultimate end, I wake each day and walk the well lit world, knowing my end won't be as quick or as painless as his.
Your memory will be a death of a million cuts

The silence

The silence of lost love, our unfinished last
conversation, the memories lost, never to lived,
the screaming of my heart for you, the quietness
that surrounds me in a busy room.
Yet my soul screams for you like a banshee
approaching the death of you and I, stentorious
noises that grip hold of my face, the cold dead
look of frosted bleakness in your eyes, burn into
me the words "it's over"

The moment

We had our "moment" on the beach
We danced our "moment" away
We spoke about our "moments" before and our "moments" ahead
We swore we would relive this "moment" again
That "moment" went like the sea pulling our time together to its darkest depths
A "moment never to be seen again
How I pray for the last moment there with you, to resurface and breath life into us again.

The tree

Remember our hill?
Watching the sun die it's day through the gnarled branches, the final rays of the days sun dancing on its ancient boughs, we made that tree come alive you and I.
Your fear? To see that tree, naked, leafless and barren.
You never got to see the tree like that.
I sit alone and see the tree everyday, looking bare and dead.
Like us, our beautiful tree's season is over

The Stars

Stargazing you and I
Each night always different yet always the same
"I can't wait to be a star" you would say to me
That's what you are now
Your a million miles away from me

The Sign

I saw a sign
"enter as strangers, leave as friends"
Such a shame that you and started as friends and
now we strangers to each other

The Stitches

Your caring hands stitched together the gaping
wounds of a former love.
Such a shame that you ripped out those stitches
with your goodbye.

The Nothing

Nothing really hurts?
The feeling of nothing.
Send a text message and get nothing.
Nothing but them in my thoughts.
Nothing but them in my heart.
Yeah, nothing really hurts!

The Burn

The sun hasn't shone for weeks now.
Nothing but darkness.
The cold winter chill, buries its self into my bones, scraping away with its icy fingers on my heart.
So cold it burns.
My body burning hot and cold.
My brain screams out for the pain to stop.
I want the burn to continue.
I would rather burn than feel the numbness I felt when you said goodbye.

The Sleep

I had the greatest sleep last night.
Best one in weeks.
You came to me in my dream.
We looked into each others eyes and our souls reconnected.
We walked.
We talked.
We laughed.
We where us again.
I was calm.
I woke up crying today.
It was the worst sleep ever.

The Rented Heart

We love with our whole heart, we give it freely to someone, we don't choose the recipient, your heart does that for you, your heart beats your brain.
But you don't actually give your heart away, you allow someone to rent space in it for as long as they want to.
Then one day, they decide that the rental agreement is up, the spaces in your heart full of their things get removed.
The feeling you get when they are gone?
That's the empty spaces they left behind.
Unoccupied, cavernous, untenanted, uninhabitable.

The Cycle

When two people meet, it's exciting and new a discovery to be made, it's perfect, people see it's perfect and you act like it's perfect.
Yet deep down you have guards up and barriers up from lost lovers and love gone wrong.
You keep them to yourself, you start off a new relationship on unsteady foundations, all the old memories stored away.
Like a marble in a shoebox, it stays still until rattled, yet once rattled the Pandora's box of frustration, self denial, awful words and abuse, explodes.
Who takes the brunt of it?
Your new love.
What have they done wrong?
Nothing.
They see you battling an unseen enemy, a battle they should have no part of, they try to help, you resist, love goes sour and the cycle begins again.

The Perfume

The worst part of not being with you, no matter where I am, you are too.
I have seen you walking the mist covered streets in front of me.
I've heard your voice while listening to the waves crashing on a pebbled beach.
I have smelled your perfume as I trudge through a forest.
I am nowhere without you, yet you have been everywhere with me.

The graveyard

Remember the night we walked the old churchyard?
We read all the tombstones, paid our respects to those who have passed on and felt sorry for the ones taken far too soon.
I walked the same graveyard alone today, same graves, same respect given, yet in one part of my mind, I was jealous of them too, they don't have to suffer anymore, suffer as I am.
I'm sure as I walked that church yard I left a part of me on each grave, tears cold and heavy as granite fell down my face, like the cold earth fell on to their coffins, their peace finally found, I so wish I was one of them.

The Gaze

Once their gaze has left your eyes
Their hands have left your grip
Their memory left your brain
Why is your heart the last thing to let go

The Call

A broken heart
A broken promise
A broken vow
A broken home
A broken you for months
A broken me for months
A broken sleep
A broken phone screen lights up
A broken voice on the line "I miss you"
A shard of sun shining through a broken cloud?

www.ingramcontent.com/pod-product-compliance
Lightning Source LLC
Chambersburg PA
CBHW051718130826
49812CB00034B/1241
* 9 7 8 9 3 5 7 2 1 2 0 0 7 *